ACKNOWLEDGEMENT

Special thanks to Dr. Shary Maskel, Executive Director of Hill Learning Center from 1985–2014; Ronni Davis; Hill Learning center faculty and staff including Jan Cirillo, Pam Hoggard, Sara Gray Horne, and Shauna Saunders; and to all of those who contributed to the development of the these readers.

ABOUT 95 RAP™

95 RAP is an individualized, small group reading intervention delivered by teachers and supported by technology and quality professional development. 95 RAP guides teachers through direct, explicit, mastery-based instruction in phonological awareness, phonics, fluency, spelling, vocabulary, and comprehension. To learn more about 95 RAP and other 95 Percent Group Products, please visit https://www.95percentgroup.com.

COPYRIGHT & PUBLISHING INFORMATION

95 Decodable Readers
Book 4

WRITTEN BY SHARON P. MASKEL, ED.D.

95 RAP™ Level: 1
Flesch-Kincaid Reading Level: Grade 1

READING LEVELS

The 95 RAP Level is aligned with the Word Attack sequence of 95 RAP and the Common Core State Standards.

The Flesch-Kincaid Grade Level Readability Formula has been assigned to each book to provide a grade level equivalency.

Source: The Flesch-Kincaid Grade Level Readability Formula
http://www.readabilityformulas.com/free-readability-formula-tests.php

Table of Contents

Chapter 1

WAT 101   CCVC Words with L-Blends (slam)

HFW 004   High Frequency Words

Stories ─────────────────────────────────────

95 Decodable Readers Book 4 • © 2022 95 Percent Group LLC

Table of Contents

Chapter 2

WAT 101   CCVC Words with L-Blends (slam)

HFW 004   High Frequency Words

Stories

Table of Contents

Chapter 3

WAT 101   CCVC Words with L-Blends (slam)

HFW 004   High Frequency Words

Stories

95 Decodable Readers Book 4 • © 2022 95 Percent Group LLC

Table of Contents

Chapter 4

WAT 101   CCVC Words with L-Blends (slam)

HFW 004   High Frequency Words

Stories

Table of Contents

Chapter 5

WAT 101   CCVC Words with L-Blends (slam)

HFW 004   High Frequency Words

Stories

Table of Contents

Chapter 6

WAT 101 CCVC Words with L-Blends (slam)

HFW 004 High Frequency Words

Stories

Table of Contents

Chapter 7

WAT 102   CCVC Words with R-Blends (Brad)

HFW 004   High Frequency Words

Stories ───────────────────────────────

Table of Contents

Chapter 8

WAT 102 CCVC Words with R-Blends (Brad)

HFW 004 High Frequency Words

Stories ───────────────────────────────

Table of Contents

Chapter 9

WAT 102   CCVC Words with R-Blends (Brad)

HFW 004   High Frequency Words

Stories

Table of Contents

Chapter 10

WAT 102   CCVC Words with R-Blends (Brad)

HFW 004   High Frequency Words

Stories ————————————————————

Table of Contents

Chapter 11

WAT 102   CCVC Words with R-Blends (Brad)

HFW 004   High Frequency Words

Stories ───────────────────────────────

Table of Contents

Chapter 12

WAT 102   CCVC Words with R-Blends (Brad)

HFW 004   High Frequency Words

Stories

Table of Contents

Chapter 13

WAT 103   CCVC Words with S-Blends (smog)

HFW 004   High Frequency Words

Stories

95 Decodable Readers Book 4 • © 2022 95 Percent Group LLC

Table of Contents

Chapter 14

WAT 103   CCVC Words with S-Blends (smog)

HFW 004   High Frequency Words

Stories ─────────────────────────────────────

Table of Contents

Chapter 15

WAT 103   CCVC Words with S-Blends (smog)

HFW 004   High Frequency Words

Stories

Table of Contents

Chapter 16

WAT 103   CCVC Words with S-Blends (smog)

HFW 004   High Frequency Words

Stories ————————————————————

Table of Contents

Chapter 17

WAT 103   CCVC Words with S-Blends (smog)

HFW 004   High Frequency Words

Stories ———————————————————————

95 Decodable Readers Book 4 • © 2022 95 Percent Group LLC

Table of Contents

Chapter 18

WAT 103   CCVC Words with S-Blends (smog)

HFW 004   High Frequency Words

Stories

Table of Contents

Chapter 19

Chapter 20

Table of Contents

Additional Content

Story Format

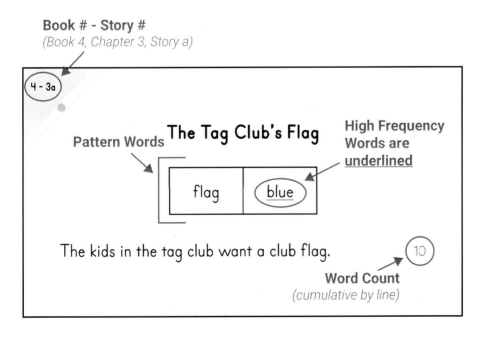

The Vet

bled

Rod's dog, Tod, likes to run and play in the sun. 11

He likes to run and run in the sun. 20

When Tod the dog ran, he cut his leg. 29

Tod got a bad cut. 34

The cut bled, so Rod fixed it. 41

He used a rag to fix it. 48

The cut was so big! 53

It bled and bled. 57

Rod had to go to the vet with Tod.   66

The vet fixed Tod's leg.   71

She fixed the cut on Tod's leg.   78

Tod, the dog, can run and play in the sun with   89

his leg fixed!   92

The Vet
Comprehension Questions

1. Who is Tod?

2. What did Rod use to fix the cut?

3. What is the problem in the story?

4. How do you think Tod felt at the end of the story?

5. Why do you think Rod took Tod to the vet?

6. What does fixed mean in the story?

    a. took care of

    b. hammered

    c. cooked

    d. brushed

7. What word does bled come from?

    a. bed

    b. bleed

    c. blue

    d. blip

Red Jam on Lips

blot

The kids beg Mom for jam. 6

Mom fixed jam for the kids. 12

They had lots of red jam. 18

The jam got all on their lips. 25

"You have red jam on your lips," said Mom. 34

"Use that rag to blot the jam from your lips," 44

she said. 46

The kids wet the rag. 51

The kids blot their lips with the wet rag. 60

They used the rag to blot their lips. 68

No more jam on their lips. 74

They are all set to go and play! 82

95 Decodable Readers Book 4 • © 2022 95 Percent Group LLC

Red Jam on Lips
Comprehension Questions

1. How did the kids get the jam off their lips?

2. What did the kids do after they got the jam off their lips?

3. What kind of jam do you think Mom fixed?

4. What do you think made the rag wet?

5. What does blot mean in the story?

    a. get wet

    b. pat dry

    c. paint with ink

    d. rub with mud

Rod Claps for Tod

clap

Rod likes to play with his dog Tod. 8

Rod can get Tod to play with him. 16

How can he get Tod to play with him? 25

If he claps, Tod will run to him and they can play. 37

Rod claps and Tod runs to him. 44

Each time Rod claps, Tod runs to him. 52

Tod the dog runs to Rod and they play. 61

When Tod runs to Rod they play and have lots of fun. 73

Rod likes to play with his dog Tod. 81

They have so much fun! 86

Rod Claps for Tod
Comprehension Questions

1. Rod likes to play with _____.

2. What happens when Rod claps?

3. What do you think is the setting of this story?

4. What do you think Rod and Tod will play?

5. What do you think they will do next?

A Clip for the Bun Bag

clip	put

Meg and Tom went for a jog. 7

They ran and ran and had a lot of fun. 17

They wanted to have hot dogs. 23

They got hot dogs. 27

They got hot dog buns. 32

"We have a lot of buns," said Meg.   40

"We can put the buns in a bag," she said.   50

Meg had a clip for the bag.   57

She put some buns in a bag and put a clip on it.   70

Meg had a clip for the bun bag.   78

Meg and Tom had hot dogs.   84

When you jog, it is fun to have hot dogs!   94

A Clip for the Bun Bag
Comprehension Questions

1.   What did Meg put in a bag?

2.   Who gets hot dogs?

3.   What do you think is the setting of the story?

 95 Decodable Readers Book 4 • © 2022 95 Percent Group LLC

Ted Digs for Clams

clam

Ted likes to dig for clams. 6

He gets wet, but it is fun for him. 15

He digs and digs for clams. 21

Ted gets lots of clams. 26

He has a big tub of clams. 33

The clams are for Mom to use. 40

She will fix the clams for Dad and Kim. 49

Mom put the clams in a big pot with a lid. 60

The clams are all set. 65

Mom, Dad, Kim, and Ted get to have lots of clams! 76

Ted Digs for Clams
Comprehension Questions

1. What does Ted like to do?

2. What does Ted put the clams in?

3. Why does Ted have to dig for clams?

4. What did Mom do with the clams?

5. What do you think Mom, Dad, Kim, and Ted did after they had clams?

6. What is a clam in this story?

    a. a toy

    b. a kind of meat

    c. a shellfish

    d. a big frog

The Tag Club

club

The kids like to play tag.   6

They run and tag a red box.   13

Can you see the kids tag the red box?   22

They tag the red box and run and run.   31

All the kids get to play.   37

They set up a tag club.   43

The kids can all play in the club.   51

The tag club uses the red box to tag.   60

The kids run and tag.   65

They have so much fun with their tag club!   74

The Tag Club
Comprehension Questions

1. What do the kids tag?

2. Who gets to play tag?

3. What do you think is the setting of the story?

4. Why do you think the kids formed a club?

5. What is a club in this story?

   a. a wooden bat

   b. a type of playing card

   c. a group of people who like the same activity

   d. a tent

The Tag Club's Flag

flag	blue

The kids in the tag club want a club flag. 10

They put a blue rag on a yellow rod. 19

They used the blue rag to make a flag. 28

It was their club flag. 33

They had a blue flag for their club. 41

They put the blue flag on top of the red box. 52

When the kids play tag, they run to the box 62

with the blue flag. 66

The kids tag the red box with the blue flag on top. 78

They tag the box with the flag and run and run. 89

They like to play tag with the red box and the 100

blue flag. 102

The tag club is fun! 107

The Tag Club's Flag
Comprehension Questions

1. Who wants a club flag?

2. What is the flag made out of?

3. Where is the flag?

4. What is the main idea of the story?

5. What is another group of people that has a flag?

6. Draw a flag with two shapes on it.

The Little Red Fox

fled

"I can see the little red fox," said Ned.   9

The little red fox was on the log.   17

He wanted to get to the hut.   24

The little red fox was set to run.   32

He fled to the hut.   37

When the fox got to the hut, two dogs were there.   48

He did not want to see them.   55

The dogs ran up to the fox.   62

The little red fox ran and ran.   69

He fled from the dogs!   74

The Little Red Fox
Comprehension Questions

1. Where was the little red fox?

2. Where did the fox go?

3. Who was at the hut?

4. What did the fox do after the dogs ran up to him?

5. What is the setting of the story?

6. What does fled mean in this story?
   a. ran away from
   b. flooded
   c. walked
   d. rained

Buns

flat

Dad wanted to make some buns for the kids. 9

The kids like hot buns. 14

Dad got a mix. 18

He was all set, but he wanted a big flat pan. 29

Dad got a big flat pan. 35

He was all set to make the buns in the big flat pan. 48

Dad mixed up the buns. 53

He put them in the big flat pan. 61

The kids had the hot buns. 67

They liked the buns a lot. 73

There are no more buns! 78

Buns
Comprehension Questions

1. Who made some buns?

2. Dad made some buns with a _____ in a _____.

3. When did the kids eat the buns?

4. Why are there no more buns?

5. What is a mix in this story?

    a. a bowl

    b. a game

    c. several ingredients

    d. several kinds of snacks

Six Hot Dogs

flip	flips

They want to have hot dogs. 6

Tom will make hot dogs for the kids. 14

How many hot dogs will Tom fix? 21

Each kid will have a hot dog. 28

There are six kids. 32

Tom will make six hot dogs. 38

He puts them in a flat pan. 45

He will use a flat pan with a lid for the hot dogs. 58

Tom flips each hot dog. 63

He flips all six hot dogs. 69

"Time for hot dogs, kids!" said Tom. 76

The six kids run from playing to have hot dogs! 86

Six Hot Dogs
Comprehension Questions

1. Who wants hot dogs?

2. Who will make hot dogs?

3. How many hot dogs will he make?

4. He used a _____ pan with a _____.

5. What are the kids doing at the beginning of the story?

6. What does flip mean in this story?

    a. turns over

    b. jumps and turns over in the air

    c. run

    d. flies

Rod and Tod Jog

glad

Rod wanted to jog with his dog Tod. 8

"It is so wet," said Rod. 14

Rod cannot jog with his dog Tod. 21

He did not want to jog with him when it is so wet. 34

When can they go? 38

Rod wanted to see the sun. 44

They can jog if there is sun. 51

"I see the sun," said Rod. 57

We can jog! 60

They like to jog in the sun. 67

Rod is so glad to see the sun. 75

Rod and Tod are so glad they can jog in the sun! 87

95 Decodable Readers Book 4 • © 2022 95 Percent Group LLC

Rod and Tod Jog
Comprehension Questions

1. Who wanted to jog?

2. At the beginning of the story, why can they not jog?

3. What happened to make it okay to jog?

4. Where do you think Rod and Tod might jog?

5. What is another word for glad?

Eat Hot Dogs

Jen	plan	glad

Jen is Mol's pal.   4

She and Mol like to eat hot dogs.   12

Jen's hot dog is small.   17

Mol's hot dog is big.   22

They plan to eat hot dogs at their spot.   31

Jen and Mol get their hats.   37

They put on their hats and the two of them   47

are set to go!   51

Jen and Mol are glad to be at their spot!   61

Eat Hot Dogs
Comprehension Questions

1. What do Jen and Mol like to do?

2. What do Jen and Mol like to wear?

3. What do you think Jen and Mol's spot is?

4. What is a pal in this story?
   a. a friend
   b. a fishing pole
   c. a fast car
   d. a fat monkey

5. What does glad mean in this story?
   a. sad
   b. fun
   c. happy

The Baby on a Jet

plan

Lan and Kim plan to go on a jet with the baby. 12

They make a plan for the baby to go on the jet. 24

Lan fed the baby. 28

The baby wants to play, but he has to have a nap. 40

"Time for a nap," Kim said to the baby. 49

"If you want to go on a jet, you have to nap," 61

said Kim. 63

She let the baby have a big nap. 71

Kim is glad that the baby has a nap. 80

When the baby has a nap, he can go on the jet. 92

He can go on the jet with Lan and Kim. 102

The baby had a big nap. 108

They are all set. 112

It will be fun for Lan, Kim, and the baby to 123

go on a jet. 127

The Baby on a Jet
Comprehension Questions

1.   What did Lan and Kim plan to do?

2.   When did Lan feed the baby?

3.   What must the baby do before she gets on the jet?

4.   Where do you think they will go on the jet?

5.   What does plan mean in this story?

     a.   ride

     b.   decide to do

     c.   forget

     d.   think

95 Decodable Readers Book 4 • © 2022 95 Percent Group LLC

Fix the Hot Rod

plug

Can Dad fix Glen's hot rod with his kit? 9

He has to plug in the kit to fix the hot rod. 21

"Get the plug," said Dad. 26

"Plug in the kit," he said to Glen. 34

Can Dad fix the hot rod with his kit? 43

He will see if it will run. 50

It runs! 52

Dad is glad he can fix Glen's hot rod with his kit. 64

Glen is glad he can go in his hot rod! 74

Fix the Hot Rod
Comprehension Questions

1. What did Dad use to fix the hot rod?

2. What did Glen do to help?

3. Did the hot rod run after Dad used his kit?

4. Why do you think Dad was glad he could fix Glen's hot rod?

5. What is a kit in this story?

    a. something electrical used to fix cars

    b. something that lifts cars

    c. something used to fix cuts

    d. something used to make dolls

Plums

plum	purple

Meg wants to get some plums. 6

"Do you like plums?" she said to Tom. 14

"Yes, I like plums," said Tom. 20

Meg went to get some plums. 26

"They have red and purple plums," said Meg. 34

"Which plums do I get?" said Meg. 41

Tom said, "I like red and purple plums." 49

Tom got red plums and purple plums. 56

He got so many! 60

We can have red plums and purple plums. 68

Tom and Meg liked the plums! 74

Plums
Comprehension Questions

1. Who wants to get plums?

2. What color are the plums?

3. Did Meg get a few plums or many plums?

4. What do you think Meg carried the plums in?

5. What is a plum in the story?

   a.   a candy

   b.   a color

   c.   a fruit

   d.   a tire

Glen Slammed the Bug

slam	slammed

Glen looked at his leg. 5

A bug had run up his leg. 12

He had a bug on his leg. 19

"I have to get that bug," Glen said. 27

He wanted to get rid of that bug. 35

"How can I get that bug?" Glen said. 43

He had a plan to get rid of that bug. 53

"I will slam that bug," he said. 60

Glen slammed the bug. 64

95 Decodable Readers Book 4 • © 2022 95 Percent Group LLC

The bug fled.   67

It ran to the rug.   72

The bug hid by the rug.   78

"I can see him," said Glen.   84

Glen used a can to get the bug.   92

"I am glad I got rid of that bug," Glen said.   103

"No more bugs can run up my leg!"   111

Glen Slammed the Bug
Comprehension Questions

1. What was Glen's plan?

2. Where did the bug hide?

3. How did Glen get the bug?

4. Where was the bug at the beginning of the story?

5. What was the problem in this story?

6. What did the bug do after Glen slammed it?

Fat Bat or Slim Bat

```
slim
```

Tim and Gus want to bat.   6

"Do you want to use a fat bat or a slim bat?"   18

said Dad.   20

"Which bat do you want to use?" said Dad.   29

"I like a fat bat," said Tim   36

"I like a slim bat," said Gus.   43

Tim bats with his fat bat.   49

Gus bats with his slim bat.   55

They each bat and get a hit.   62

When they get a hit, they run to the bags.   72

Tim and Gus run to the bags.   79

Tim and Gus like to bat and have fun!   88

Fat Bat or Slim Bat
Comprehension Questions

1. What do Tim and Gus want to do?

2. What kinds of bats are there in this story?

3. What happens after Tim and Gus bat?

4. What do you think Tim and Gus will do next?

5. What does slim mean in the story?

    a. hard

    b. thin

    c. long

    d. fat

6. What are bags in this story?

    a. suitcases

    b. sacks

    c. bases

    d. boxes

A Little Jog

slip

Pam and Meg want to jog.   6

It is so wet.   10

When it is so wet, there is a lot of mud.   21

They do not want to go when it is so wet.   32

Pam and Meg do not want to slip in the mud.   43

"Can we go if there is a little mud?" said Pam.   54

"There is a little mud and some sun," said Meg.   64

"We can go if there is a little mud and some sun,"   76

said Pam.   78

It is not so bad.   83

They will not slip in the mud.   90

Pam and Meg go for a little jog!   98

A Little Jog
Comprehension Questions

1. Why is there a lot of mud?

2. What do Pam and Meg not want to do?

3. What is the setting of this story?

4. How will the sun help?

5. What do you think Pam and Meg will do next?

 95 Decodable Readers Book 4 • © 2022 95 Percent Group LLC

Tim and Bob Slid

slid

Tim and Bob like to bat. 6

They play a lot with their bats. 13

Tim has his fat bat. 18

Bob has his slim bat. 23

They like to go to bat, and run to the bags. 34

Tim bats with his fat bat and runs. 42

Can he get to the bag? 48

He slid to the bag. 53

95 Decodable Readers Book 4 • © 2022 95 Percent Group LLC

Bob bats with his slim bat and runs. 61

Can he get to the bag? 67

He slid to the bag. 72

Tim and Bob slid to the bags. 79

They like to bat and have fun! 86

Tim and Bob Slid
Comprehension Questions

1. How did Tim and Bob get to the bags?

2. Who are the characters in this story?

3. Who bats and runs first?

4. What game are Tim and Bob playing?

5. What does slid mean in this story?

    a. bumped

    b. moved smoothly

    c. ran

    d. crawled

Sledding

sled	sledding

Sid has a red sled.   5

He likes to go sledding.   10

He slid from the top of the rim.   18

Sid met his pal Brad.   23

Brad has a blue sled.   28

Brad and Sid run and hop on their sleds.   37

They go like jets on their sleds.   44

The two have so much fun!   50

They like to play on their sleds.   57

Sledding
Comprehension Questions

1. What does Sid have?

2. Where does Sid start from?

3. What color is Brad's sled?

4. What is the setting of the story?

5. What does "like jets" mean in this story?

   a. very bumpy

   b. very fast

   c. very cold

   d. very hot

Brad's Hat

brim	rubbed	yellow	purple

Brad got a hat. 4

It fits, but it is a little big. 12

The hat is yellow, but the brim is purple. 21

"The brim is so flat," said Brad. 28

"I can fix it," his mom said. 35

Mom rubbed on the brim of the hat. 43

She fixed the brim of his hat so it fit. 53

It is not flat. 57

Brad likes his hat. 61

He can use it when he bats. 68

Brad's Hat
Comprehension Questions

1. What did Brad get?

2. What colors are the hat?

3. What is the problem with the hat?

4. How did Mom fix the hat?

5. When does Brad wear his hat?

6. What is a brim in this story?

    a. the rim of a hat

    b. a fish

    c. a body of water

    d. an edge of something

Blue Crabs

crab	crabs

Dad wanted to get some blue crabs. 7

He would have to dig for the crabs. 15

Dad makes a plan to get the crabs. 23

He gets a net. 27

He gets a tub. 31

Dad will get the crabs and put them in the tub. 42

95 Decodable Readers Book 4 • © 2022 95 Percent Group LLC

The crabs run and dig.   47

Some of the crabs slip by him, but he got two.   58

How many did he get in all?   65

Dad got ten crabs.   69

He will put the crabs in a big pot with a lid.   81

Dad and the kids all like to have blue crabs.   91

Blue Crabs
Comprehension Questions

1. How would Dad get the crabs?

2. What will Dad need to catch the crabs?

3. What do the crabs do?

4. How many crabs did Dad catch?

5. Where did Dad put the crabs?

95 Decodable Readers Book 4 • © 2022 95 Percent Group LLC

A Crib for the Baby

crib	white	blue	yellow	purple

Ben and Pam want to get a crib for their baby. 11

They go to look at cribs. 17

Do they want a yellow crib? 23

Do they want a blue crib? 29

Do they want a red crib? 35

Do they want a purple crib? 41

They want a white crib for their baby. 49

They get a white crib for the baby. 57

Pam is so glad. 61

She put the baby in the white crib. 69

Look! I can see the baby clap in his white crib! 80

A Crib for the Baby
Comprehension Questions

1. What do Ben and Pam want to get?

2. What color crib did they get?

3. What do you think is the setting for this story?

4. What did the baby do at the end of the story?

5. Why do you think Pam is glad?

A Log in the Mud

drag	dragged	nip

The dogs like to play at the dog pen. 9

It is so wet by the dog pen. 17

They run and slip in the mud by the pen. 27

The dogs get a little log. 33

They nip at the log. 38

They like to drag it in the mud. 46

The dogs drag it to the dog pen. 54

The dogs played with the little log. 61

They dragged the log in the mud to the dog pen. 72

The dogs have fun with the little log, in the mud, 83

by the dog pen. 87

A Log in the Mud
Comprehension Questions

1. What is the weather like?

2. What do the dogs do with the log?

3. What might the dogs play with other than a log?

4. How is mud made?

5. What does nip mean in this story?
   a. drink
   b. bite
   c. kick
   d. tickle

A Dropped Hot Dog

drop	dropped

Ben and Tim met to jog.   6

They ran and ran.   10

They had a big run.   15

"I want a hot dog," said Ben.   22

"I can fix us hot dogs," said Tim.   30

Tim got hot dogs and buns. 36

He put the hot dog on the bun for Ben, but it slipped. 49

Did he drop the hot dog? 55

It dropped on his bun. 60

"I have my hot dog," said Ben. 67

Ben was glad he got his hot dog. 75

Tim fixed hot dogs for them. 81

Tim and Ben jogged and had their hot dogs. 90

A Dropped Hot Dog
Comprehension Questions

1. Why did Ben and Tom meet?

2. What did Ben want to eat?

3. What happened to the hot dog?

4. What do you think Tim and Ben will do next?

5. What does dropped mean in this story?

    a. fell

    b. smashed

    c. sat

    d. stood

Glen Plays Drums

drum

Glen has a drum set. 5

He likes to hit each of the drums. 13

Glen likes to play the drums. 19

He plans to play for the kids. 26

He is set to play the drums for the kids on Sunday. 38

The kids beg him to play his drums. 46

Glen plays for the kids. 51

The kids like him and his drums. 58

They clap and clap for Glen. 64

He is hot on the drums! 70

Glen has lots of fun with his drums. 78

95 Decodable Readers Book 4 • © 2022 95 Percent Group LLC

Glen Plays Drums
Comprehension Questions

1. How does Glen play the drums?

2. When did Glen play the drums?

3. Why do the kids clap?

4. What is a drum set in this story?

   a. a group

   b. a cover

   c. a stick

   d. a hat

5. What does hot mean in this story?

   a. warm

   b. hot

   c. great

   d. sad

On a Jet

Fran	Fred	orange

Fran and Fred plan to go on a jet. 9

They will go on Sunday. 14

It is time to go. 19

Fran and Fred are set to go on the orange jet. 30

They have their bags. 34

Fred's bag is blue and Fran's bag is purple. 43

Fran and Fred are all set to go. 51

They have two bags. 55

"Let the man have the bags," said Fran. 63

Fred slid the bags to the man. 70

He had a tip for him. 76

The orange jet will go up and up. 84

I bet they will have fun. 90

Fran and Fred will have lots of fun on the orange jet! 102

On a Jet
Comprehension Questions

1. When will Fran and Fred go on a jet?

2. What color is the jet?

3. How many bags do Fran and Fred have?

4. How do you think Fran and Fred will have fun?

5. What is a tip in this story?

   a. a point

   b. a suggestion

   c. money

   d. a sharp point

Ben Gets Rid of the Bug

fret

"I see a big bug by the orange rug," said Mom.   11

Mom wanted to get that bug.   17

"Do not fret, Mom," said Ben.   23

"I can get that bug," Ben said.   30

"When he runs, I will slam that bug."   38

The bug by the orange rug fled.   45

Ben ran and ran to get that bug.   53

Can Ben nab him?   57

Ben slams the bug.   61

Mom is glad that Ben got rid of that big bug!   72

Ben Gets Rid of the Bug
Comprehension Questions

1. What did Mom see?

2. How did Ben get the bug?

3. Why do you think Mom wanted to get rid of the bug?

4. What does nab mean in this story?

    a. hit

    b. eat

    c. catch

    d. run

Babs Has Catnip

grin	catnip

Cats like catnip.   3

Babs the cat wants some catnip.   9

Can she have some catnip?   14

Meg gave Babs some catnip.   19

When she has catnip her lips go up.   27

It looks like she has a grin for Meg.   36

Babs is so glad to have catnip.   43

"Hop up on my lap," said Meg.   50

Meg pets Babs.   53

She rubs and rubs Babs.   58

Meg likes her cat, Babs, a lot!   65

Babs Has Catnip
Comprehension Questions

1. Who gave Babs some catnip?

2. How does catnip make Babs feel?

3. Where did Babs sit?

4. How do you think Babs felt when Meg rubbed her?

5. What is the main idea of the story?

The Kids Play Tag

grab	planned

The kids planned to play tag. 6

They had to set up the yellow box with the blue flag. 18

"Grab the box," said one of the kids. 26

"Drag it to the tag lot," said Ben. 34

They slid the box to the tag lot. 42

"Let me put the blue flag on it," said Ben. 52

He set up the box with the blue flag. 61

They were set to play tag and they did. 70

The kids had fun. 74

They like to play tag at the tag lot! 83

95 Decodable Readers Book 4 • © 2022 95 Percent Group LLC

The Kids Play Tag
Comprehension Questions

1. What did the kids use in tag?

2. What is the setting of the story?

3. What happened before the kids put the blue flag on the box?

4. Why do you think they put the flag on the box?

5. What does slid mean in this story?

   a. lifted

   b. dragged

   c. rolled

   d. fell

A Trap

trap	trapped	tugged	slipped

The red fox tugged at his pen. 7

He fled from his pen. 12

The red fox ran and ran. 18

The men have to get the fox. 25

They want to trap him. 30

They have to set up a trap to get the red fox. 42

95 Decodable Readers Book 4 • © 2022 95 Percent Group LLC

The fox hid from the men.   48

They set up a big trap for him.   56

They wanted to trap him and get him in his pen.   67

They set up the trap to get the red fox.   77

The fox ran into the trap.   83

The men were glad to trap the fox.   91

The fox slipped into his pen.   97

The fox is in his pen!   103

A Trap
Comprehension Questions

1. How did the fox get out of his pen?

2. What did the men want to do?

3. Why did the men set a trap?

4. What is the setting of this story?

5. What does slipped mean in this story?

   a. ran

   b. fell

   c. went quietly

   d. walked

95 Decodable Readers Book 4 • © 2022 95 Percent Group LLC

A Nap for Fred

trip

Fran and Fred had lots of fun on their trip.　　10

Their trip on the orange jet was fun.　　18

They did lots on their trip, but they were glad　　28

to sit a bit.　　32

They had their bags.　　36

They got into a yellow cab.　　42

95 Decodable Readers Book 4 • © 2022 95 Percent Group LLC

Fred wanted to have a nap in the cab.   51

"I have to have a nap, Fran," said Fred.   60

Fran had a grin for Fred.   66

"It is time for you to have a nap, Fred, " said Fran.   79

Fred was glad to have a nap.   86

They did have fun, but it was time to nap!   96

A Nap for Fred
Comprehension Questions

1. How did Fran and Fred travel?

2. Why do you think Fred had to have a nap?

3. What do you think Fran and Fred will do next?

4. Where might Fran and Fred have gone on their trip?

5. What are bags in this story?
   a. suitcases
   b. sacks
   c. purses
   d. toys

The Dogs Trot

trot	trotted

Rod and Tod's dogs like to jog.   7

The dogs run and run.   12

Rod and Tod would like for their dogs to trot.   22

They want the dogs to trot, not run.   30

"We can trot with the dogs," said Rod.   38

When the dogs trot, not run, we can pet them.   48

We will pet the dogs when they trot.   56

95 Decodable Readers Book 4 • © 2022 95 Percent Group LLC

Rod and Tod trot with their dogs. 63

With time, the dogs can trot, not run. 71

The dogs trotted and did not run! 78

Rod and Tod are glad that the dogs can trot, 88

not run and run! 92

The Dogs Trot
Comprehension Questions

1.   What do the dogs like to do?

2.   What can Rod and Tod do when the dogs trot?

3.   What is the setting of this story?

4.   Where do you think the dogs are going?

5.   What does trot mean in this story?

   a.   run fast

   b.   run slowly

   c.   crawl

   d.   skip

Ben's Tin Top

spin	spun

"What is in the box?" said Ben. 7

"It is for you," said Mom. 13

Ben looked in the box. 18

It was a tin top. 23

"What can you do with a tin top?" said Ben. 33

"A top can spin," said Mom. 39

Ben spun the tin top. 44

"See the top spin and spin," said Ben. 52

Ben likes his tin top. 57

It is fun to spin the tin top! 65

95 Decodable Readers Book 4 • © 2022 95 Percent Group LLC

Ben's Tin Top
Comprehension Questions

1.   What is in the box?

2.   What did Ben do with the top?

3.   Who are the characters in this story?

4.   Where do you think Mom got the top?

5.   What is tin in this story?

   a.   a metal

   b.   silver

   c.   sharp

   d.   food

A Black Spot

spot	black

"There is a black spot on the white rug," said Dad. 11

"I can see it is a big spot," he said. 21

What can Dad do? 25

He wants the black spot to go. 32

"I will have to wet the rug," said Dad. 41

"If I wet it and rub it, that will make the spot go. 54

It is a big job to make that spot go, but he did it. 68

Dad rubbed and rubbed. 72

He had to blot the wet spot. 79

He will put the rug flat. 85

Dad is glad to see that spot go! 93

A Black Spot
Comprehension Questions

1. What was on the rug?

2. How did Dad fix the spot?

3. Why was Dad glad at the end of the story?

4. What do you think made the black spot?

5. What does blot mean in this story?

   a. wet

   b. dry

   c. cut

   d. tap

Glen Plays Drums

sped

Bob was in his hot rod. 6

Glen wanted to go to the Kids' Club. 14

"Can I go with you?" said Glen. 21

Glen wanted Bob to drop him at the Kids' Club. 31

"I can drop you at the Kids' Club," said Bob. 41

It was time to go. 46

Glen had to play the drums at the Kids' Club.   56

Bob sped to the club in his hot rod.   65

He wanted to get Glen there in time.   73

Glen got to the Kids' Club on time.   81

He was so glad to play drums for the kids.   91

The kids clap for Glen when he plays the drums.   101

It was fun for Glen and the kids!   109

Glen Plays Drums
Comprehension Questions

1. Where was Bob?

2. Who wanted to go with Bob?

3. Why did Bob speed to the club?

4. What did Glen do at the Kids' Club?

5. What does sped mean in this story?

    a. drove slowly

    b. rolled

    c. drove fast

    d. stopped

Lan Can Fix the Big Rig

stop	stopped

The big rig was on a job. 7

Lan was in his van. 12

Lan had to go to the big rig to fix it. 23

He had a plan to fix it. 30

Lan had to get a map to get to the rig. 41

He planned to go to the rig, but he had to get a kit. 55

He had to stop and get a kit to fix the rig. 67

95 Decodable Readers Book 4 • © 2022 95 Percent Group LLC

"What kit do I get?" said Lan to the man.   77

The man said to get a big kit for that big rig.   89

Lan got the big kit.   94

He got into his van to go to the big rig.   105

Lan stopped at the rig to fix it.   113

He used the kit to fix the big rig.   122

He can make the rig work with his kit.   131

Lan was so glad to fix the big rig!   140

Lan Can Fix the Big Rig
Comprehension Questions

1. How did Lan get to the rig?

2. What did Lan need to get?

3. How did Lan feel at the end of the story?

4. What do you think was in the kit?

5. What is a rig in the story?

    a.   a ship

    b.   a building

    c.   a truck

    d.   a boat

Stan's Drums

Stan	step

Stan liked to play the drums. 6

The kids would beg him to play for them. 15

Stan liked to play pop. 20

Stan would play pop for the kids at the Kids' Club. 31

Stan would play his red drums for the kids. 40

The kids would hop to the drums. 47

They would step to the drums. 53

The kids would tap to the drums. 60

They would spin to the drums. 66

The kids would hop, step, tap and spin to the drums. 77

It was so much fun! 82

They like for Stan to play his red drums. 91

Stan's Drums
Comprehension Questions

1. What did the kids beg Stan to do?

2. What kind of music did Stan play?

3. What did the kids do when Stan played the drums?

4. Where do you think Stan played his drums?

5. What does beg mean in this story?

    a. tell

    b. sing

    c. ask

    d. whisper

Brown Smog

smog	planning	brown

Stan and Pam are planning a trip. 7

They wanted to go in Stan's van. 14

"The brown smog is so bad," said Stan. 22

"Can we go when there is no more brown smog?" 32
he said. 34

Pam said, "Yes, let us go when there is no more 45
brown smog." 47

"What if we go when it is wet?" said Stan. 57

It was so wet on Sunday. 63

It was so wet and there was no more brown smog. 74

Stan and Pam are glad that there is no more 84
brown smog. 86

Stan and Pam can go on their trip! 94

Brown Smog
Comprehension Questions

1. What are Stan and Pam planning to do?

2. Why did Stan want to go away?

3. When was it wet?

4. What do you think Stan and Pam will do on their trip?

5. What is smog in this story?

   a. dirt

   b. fog

   c. car exhaust

   d. rain

Smug Ben

smug

Ben wanted to go to the Kids' Club. 8

Mom said no to Ben. 13

You have to do a job. 19

"You have not fed the dog," said Mom. 27

Ben was smug. 30

He wanted to go to the Kids' Club. 38

"If the dog is fed, you can go," said Mom. 48

With a grin, Ben fed the dog. 55

"You did that job," said Mom. 61

"You can go to the Kids' Club! 68

95 Decodable Readers Book 4 • © 2022 95 Percent Group LLC

Smug Ben
Comprehension Questions

1. What did Ben want to do?

2. What was Ben's job?

3. How did Ben feel? How can you tell?

4. What do you think Ben will do at the Kids' Club?

5. What does smug mean in this story?

   a. hurt

   b. mad

   c. satisfied

   d. angry

A Green Snap Cap

snap	green

Stan wanted a hat for when he played the drums.   10

His drums were red, but he wanted a green cap.   20

He would play his red drums with his green cap.   30

Stan got a green cap with a snap.   38

You can snap the brim of the cap.   46

It is a rad snap cap!   52

Stan went to the Kids' Club with his green snap cap.   63

"How do I look?" said Stan.   69

The kids said, "You are rad, Stan!"   76

Stan played the drums at the Kids' Club with   85

his green snap cap!   89

A Green Snap Cap
Comprehension Questions

1. What instrument did Stan play?

2. What did Stan get?

3. How did Stan look?

4. What is a brim in this story?

    a. the front of a cap

    b. the top of a cap

    c. a snap on a cap

    d. a tag on a cap

5. What does rad mean in this story?

    a. ugly

    b. cool

    c. huge

    d. baby stuff

Snug As a Bug in a Rug

snug	jogging

Tim and his pup Gus went jogging.   7

When they jogged, Gus had to have a nap.   16

Gus wanted to have a big nap.   23

Gus got on his rug.   28

Tim's pup, Gus, had a big nap.   35

Tim sees him nap.   39

He grins at Gus.   43

He is as snug as a bug in a rug!   53

Snug As a Bug in a Rug
Comprehension Questions

1. Where did Gus nap?

2. What is the setting in this story?

3. Why do you think Gus had to have a nap?

4. Why do you think Tim grinned at Gus?

5. What does snug mean in this story?

   a. warm

   b. comfortable

   c. fast

   d. hot

Brad Got Cut

scab

Brad was playing on a big log.	7
He wanted to step up on top of the log.	17
Can he make a big step onto the log?	26
No, Brad slipped on the log.	32
He hit the log with his leg.	39
Brad's leg was cut.	43
He had a big cut on his leg.	51
It bled and bled.	55
Brad was sad.	58
Mom can blot the cut and fix it.	66

Mom said, "You may get a scab on that leg   76

from the cut."   79

"No more playing on that big log," said Brad.   88

Brad Got Cut
Comprehension Questions

1. What is the problem in this story?

2. What happened after Brad stepped onto the log?

3. Why do you think Brad was sad?

4. What do you think Mom used to blot the cut?

5. What is a scab in this story?

    a. a cut

    b. a scar

    c. dried blood

    d. a scratch

Tom Can Scan

scan	scanned	scanner

Tom wanted to scan some words. 6

"Do you have time to scan this for me, Dad?" 16

said Tom. 18

"Can you scan the words here?" Tom said to Dad. 28

Dad said,"I can fix it so you can scan that." 38

"You can do it, Tom," said Dad. 45

He got it all fixed for Tom. 52

Tom scanned the words. 56

He is glad that he can use the scanner. 65

Tom is all set. 69

He can scan his words! 74

 95 Decodable Readers Book 4 • © 2022 95 Percent Group LLC

Tom Can Scan
Comprehension Questions

1. What did Tom want to do?

2. What did Dad do for Tom?

3. How do you think Tom felt at the end of the story?

4. What does scan mean in this story?

    a.   look at

    b.   read the price of

    c.   copy an image of

    d.   write on

5. What does "all set" mean in this story?

    a.   ready

    b.   sitting

    c.   happy

    d.   sad

Play Time

skip

The kids do not want to sit.   7

They want to have play time.   13

"What can we do, Mom?" said the kids.   21

"Can we skip?" said the kids. "Yes, you can skip,"   31

said Mom.   33

"Can we hop?" said the kids. "Yes, you can hop,"   43

said Mom.   45

"Can we run?" said the kids. "Yes, you can run,"   55

said Mom.   57

"Can we flip?" said the kids. "Yes, you can flip,"   67

said Mom.   69

"Can we spin?" said the kids. "Yes, we can spin,"   79

said Mom.   81

"We can do a lot," said the kids.   89

The kids can skip, hop, run, flip, and spin.   98

When the kids play, they all spin, flip, run, hop,   108

and spin.   110

The kids are glad it is time to play.   119

They have lots of fun!   124

Play Time
Comprehension Questions

1. How can the kids move?

2. How do the kids feel at the end of the story?

3. Who are the characters in this story?

4. Where do you think the kids flip?

5. What is the word that means a way of moving like a run with a hop?

   a. flip

   b. skip

   c. spin

   d. jump

 95 Decodable Readers Book 4 • © 2022 95 Percent Group LLC

A Hot Run

skin

Ned and Ben were going for a jog.   8

Ben said, "I like to jog, but it is so hot."   19

"It is so hot in the sun," he said.   28

"We can go on a little run," said Ned.   37

Ned and Ben go on a little run.   45

Ned said, "Ben, your skin is red from the sun."   55

Ben said, "Ned, your skin is red from the sun."   65

They are so hot from the sun.   72

Their skin is hot and red from the sun.   81

They stop their jogging.   85

It is so hot in the sun.   92

It is fun to run in the sun, but not when it is so hot!   107

A Hot Run
Comprehension Questions

1.   What were Ned and Ben doing?

2.   Why is their skin red?

3.   What is the main idea of this story?

4.   What do you think Ned and Ben will do next?

5.   What does jogging mean in this story?

    a.   swimming

    b.   walking

    c.   running

    d.   skipping

The Kids' Skit

$$\boxed{\text{skit}}$$

The kids planned to do a skit.   7

Dad will go in the van with the kids.   16

They all got in the van to go.   24

They met at the Kids' Club.   30

When they got there, the kids wanted to play.   39

"It is time to set up for the skit," said Dad.   50

The kids set up for the skit.   57

Stan got his red drum.   62

Ben put on his white wig.   68

Pam is set to tap and flip.   75

95 Decodable Readers Book 4 • © 2022 95 Percent Group LLC

The kids do their skit.   80

The skit is fun for the kids.   87

They are glad to put on a skit.   95

All the kids clap!   99

The Kids' Skit
Comprehension Questions

1. What did the kids want to do?

2. What did Dad tell them to do?

3. What did Ben wear?

4. What did Pam do in the skit?

5. Why did the kids clap?

6. What is a skit in this story?

    a. a skip

    b. a short play

    c. a song

    d. a dance

95 Decodable Readers Book 4 • © 2022 95 Percent Group LLC

A Swim at the Kids Club

swim

It is hot. 3

The kids want to play, but they are so hot! 13

Dad can fix up a tub for the kids to sit in. 25

The kids sit in the big tub. 32

The kids were in the big tub, but it got hot. 43

The big tub got so hot! 49

"Can we go for a swim at the Kids' Club?" said Ben.   61

It is so hot that the kids want to go for a swim.   74

"Yes," said Dad.   77

"You can swim at the Kids' Club."   84

The kids got in the van to go to the Kids' Club.   96

It will be fun to swim when it is so hot.   107

The kids like to swim and play when it is so hot!   119

A Swim at the Kids Club
Comprehension Questions

1. What did Dad fix up for the kids to sit in?

2. How did the kids get to the Kid's Club?

3. What is the problem in this story?

4. Why do you think the big tub got hot?

5. What do you think the kids will play in the pool?

Kids Swam

swam	tagged

The kids swam at the Kids' Club. 7

It was hot, but they did have fun. 15

They had lots of fun in the sun at the Kids' Club. 27

They swam and they played tag. 33

They would tag kids, and they would run and swim. 43

The kids would spin, flip, and flop not to get tagged. 54

When it is so hot, it is fun to swim and play tag. 67

The kids are not so hot when they swim. 76

They swam and swam and had a lot of fun! 86

Kids Swam
Comprehension Questions

1. What did the kids do at the Kids' Club?

2. How did the kids keep from getting tagged?

3. What season do you think it is? Why?

4. How do you think the water feels?

5. What does tagged mean in this story?

   a. put a tag on

   b. named

   c. touched

   d. pinched

Tad Can Slug It

slug	slugged

Tad is at bat.   4

He wants to have a big hit and slug it.   14

Tad gets set to hit.   19

He gets a hit!   23

Tad slugged it.   26

He runs and runs.   30

Tad tags the bags as he runs.   37

Tad is so glad he got a big hit.   46

He can slug it!   50

I can see Tad has a big grin.   58

 95 Decodable Readers Book 4 • © 2022 95 Percent Group LLC

Tad Can Slug It
Comprehension Questions

1. What does Tad want to do?

2. How does Tad feel?

3. What is on Tad's face?

4. What did Tad do after he slugged the ball?

5. What is the main idea of this story?

6. What do you think Tad will do next?

7. What does slug mean in this story?

   a. insect

   b. slow-moving

   c. hit

   d. drag

The Rat That Hid

flag

The rat hid in the grid.   6

The rat hid in the hat.   12

The rat hid by the hat.   18

The rat hid by the flag.   24

Where is the rat?   28

The rat hid in the club.   34

The rat hid in the slit.   40

The rat hid by the plum.   46

Where is the rat?   50

The rat hid from the cat!   56

The Rat That Hid
Comprehension Questions

1. Where did the rat hide?

2. Why did the rat hide?

3. Why did the rat hide in so many different places?

4. What is a grid in this story?

    a. a piece of wood

    b. a girl's name

    c. a wooden marble

    d. a maze with twists and turns

Brad Swims

scab	swam

Brad is on a trip with his mom. 8

It is hot on the trip. 14

"Let's swim!" Brad says with a grin. 21

Brad and his mom go to swim. 28

Brad slips and skids. 32

He gets a scab. 36

Mom hugs Brad. "Don't fret. It's a little scab." 45

Brad and his mom swam. 50

Then they were not hot. 55

95 Decodable Readers Book 4 • © 2022 95 Percent Group LLC

Brad Swims
Comprehension Questions

1. Where is Brad?

2. How is the weather?

3. Why did Brad want to swim?

4. What is the problem in this story?

5. What happens to Brad when he slips?

6. What does fret mean in this story?
    a.   to smile
    b.   to get upset
    c.   to complain
    d.   to laugh

Review Phonetic Words

crab	grab	rubbed	dropped
jogging	sled	club	put
stopped	flips	grin	brim
Stan	spot	plug	bled
flag	flip	trap	slam
slugged	crib	slipped	blot
tagged	plum	Fran	skip
slim	drag	spun	stop
sped	swim	slip	catnip
fled	scab	Jen	drum
smog	snap	nip	planning
drop	sledding	glad	slid
slammed	clap	spin	dragged
plan	smug	step	clam
scanned	fret	clip	skit
scan	crabs	flat	snug
trip	scanner	slug	tugged
planned	trotted	skin	Fred
swam	trapped	trot	

Total Phonetic Words: 75

Review High Frequency Words

yellow	white	purple	brown
orange	black	blue	green

Made in United States
North Haven, CT
01 April 2025

67475555R00091